SHIRLEY BASSEY

JOHN EVANS

Illustrated by Malcolm Stokes

DREF WEN

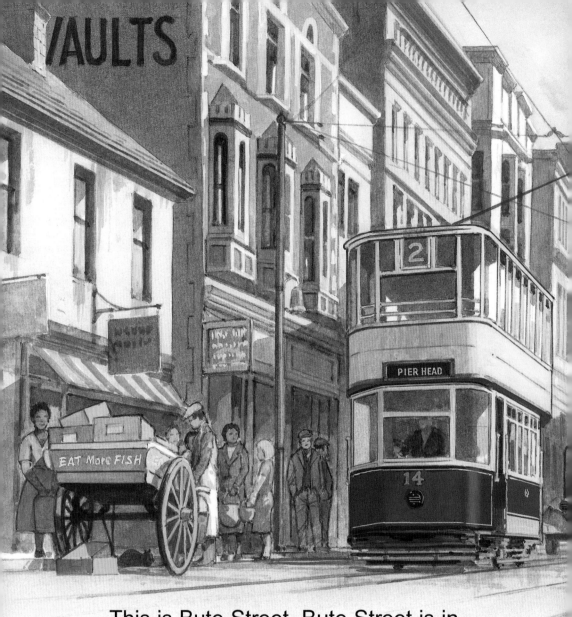

This is Bute Street. Bute Street is in Cardiff. On 8th January 1937, a famous singer was born in number 182. Her name was Shirley Bassey.

The family was very poor. Shirley was the
youngest child of seven. She never had
any new clothes to wear. She always had
to wear her big sisters' old clothes.

At that time, the part of Cardiff where Shirley lived was called Tiger Bay. It was where the ships came to take coal from Wales to all parts of the world. Shirley's father was a sailor from Africa.

One day, when Shirley was only two years old, her father sailed away and she never saw him again. Shirley's mother was left alone to look after her seven children.

Shirley did not like her life in Tiger Bay.
She did not like being poor. She did not like
school. But she did like singing.

At parties she would sing for threepence.
She was so shy, she used to hide under
the table to sing.

Shirley left school when she was fifteen
years old. She went to work in a factory.
Her job was to pack saucepans into boxes.
It was a very boring job.

Shirley liked listening to records of
Judy Garland, and she liked going to the
pictures. She saw a film called 'The
Wizard of Oz'. The star of the film was
Judy Garland. Shirley thought, "I want to
be a famous singer like Judy."

On Saturday nights, Shirley sang in clubs
in Cardiff to earn some more money. One
night, a man asked her to come and sing
in his show. He said, "Give up your job
and come and work for me."

She worked for a year as a singer and travelled all over the country. But life was hard, and she had to return home to Cardiff.

One day, she received a telegram from a man who owned a theatre in London. It said, "I need you to work in my new show." People had not forgotten Shirley's beautiful voice.

Shirley had to go to London for a special
test called an audition. She arrived wearing
an old pair of jeans and a dirty jumper.
The people at the theatre did not like her
at first. But when she started to sing,
they knew that Shirley would be a Star.

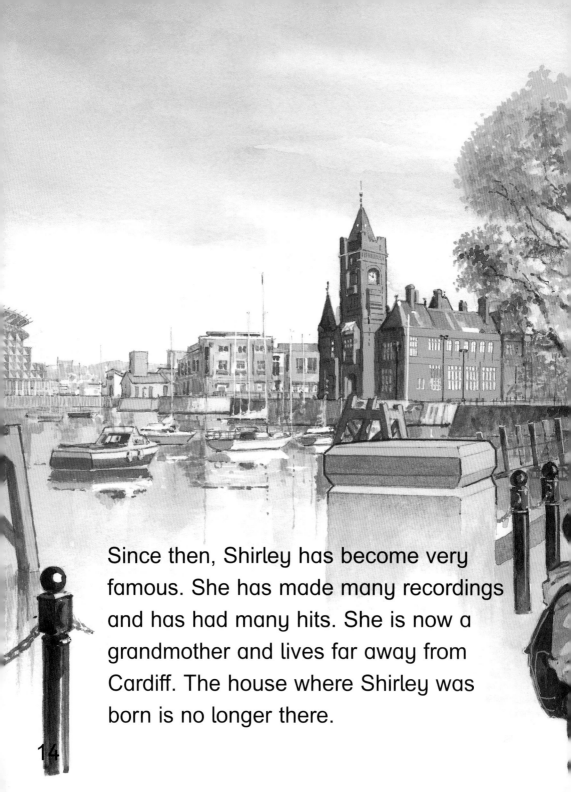

Since then, Shirley has become very famous. She has made many recordings and has had many hits. She is now a grandmother and lives far away from Cardiff. The house where Shirley was born is no longer there.

In Concert

Shirley Bassey

and special guest

at

CARDIFF CASTLE

It is difficult for her to remember how it used to be, because Tiger Bay is changing so much. But when she returns to sing, everyone remembers Shirley and thousands come to hear her sing.

INDEX